MY OWN SILENCE

poems

JEANNE POWELL

Taurean Horn Press
Petaluma, CA

copyright © 2014 by Jeanne Powell
http://jeanne-powell.com

ALL RIGHTS RESERVED

No part of this book may be reproduced or transmitted in any form or by any means, electronic or mechanical, including photocopying, recording, or by any information storage and retrieval system, without permission in writing from the author.

published by

**Taurean Horn Press
Petaluma, California**

Second Edition

ISBN 978-0-931552-18-2

Photos on cover by Jeanne Powell

Abstract drawings by Q.R. Hand, Jr.
Used by permission

ACKNOWLEDGEMENTS

"A True Story" in SACRED GROUNDS ANTHOLOGY #8, Minotaur Press, Oakland CA, 2001.

"War *Haiku*" in SACRED GROUNDS ANTHOLOGY #12, Minotaur Press, Oakland CA, 2003 and CAVEAT LECTOR, San Francisco, 2004.

"Cooper's Hawk" *haiku* in RAW NERVZ quarterly, Canada, summer 2002.

"Red Shoes" in THE THROWBACK annual, San Francisco, 2004.

"When I Was Just A Little Girl" in NORTH COAST REVIEW, vol. 1, from Penzance Press, San Francisco, 2004.

"Next Time" (1) won first place in the Paul Lawrence Dunbar poetry contest sponsored by Detroit Writers Guild 2002; and (2) appeared in PO annual, TreeFree Press, www.Gg-Re.org, 2005.

"Journey" in SACRED GROUNDS ANTHOLOGY #8, Minotaur Press, Oakland CA, 2001.

"East Bay Miracle" in DRUMVOICES REVUE tenth anniversary issue, vol. 11, nos. 1 & 2, Southern Illinois University at Edwardsville, 2003.

Selected for Creative Justice Arts Exhibition, University of San Francisco, Kendrick Hall, February 2006: "Next Time," "If the Shoe Fits," and "Making Amends."

CONTENTS

My Own Silence *Haiku*…11
The Silence…13
The Time It Was…14
When I Was Just A Little Girl…15-16
A Good Child [1997]…17
Puppy Love…18
End of Ceremony…19
Journey….20
Ribbons I…27
Ribbons II…28
Coffee Talk…29
On The Wire…30
Enter Laughing…31
A Walk in the Park…32
Beans…33
Witsteria…34
Misled By A Rose…41
Rosemary…42
To Stay the Night…43
Five O'Clock…44
The Lost Prince…45
Denial…46
Red Shoes…47
Confession…48
Old Believers…49
History Lesson…50
September 12, 2001…57
Ordinary People…58
Sunset Bar…59-60

CONTENTS

If The Shoe Fits...61-62
Next Time...63
East Bay Miracle...64-65
A True Story...66
Last Call...67-68
On Sarajevo Time (1992-1995)...69
Trouble In Mind...70
Postmortem 2000...71
November 3, 2004...72
Making Amends...73-75
This Is A Love Poem...83-84
A Gratitude Poem...85
Haiku...86-105
About the author...107

BOOKS BY JEANNE POWELL

CAROUSEL
(Essays & Such)
[Regent Press]

WORD DANCING
(Prose Poems and Collages)
[Taurean Horn Press]

MY OWN SILENCE
(Prose Poems and Haiku)
[Taurean Horn Press]

TWO SEASONS
(Poetry Chapbook)
[Meridien PressWorks]

what to discard
manufactured dreams
my own silence

    - for Lydia

THE SILENCE

Mama, why didn't you leave him?
silence
moving in circles
muscular arms
scrub   clean   disinfect
window sills, life times

Why did you stay, Mama?
silence
what price
rivulets of sweat stream down
drip, marking steel surfaces

You could leave him now, Mama.
stillness
twisting in her mother's throat
the howl spills out, splashing
quicksilver
muscular

mute child
crouches on a closet floor
wordless screams rain down
her long shiny braids
bounce this way, that way
in the drenching
waiting for the sky to clear

THE TIME IT WAS

be quiet – you're making too much noise
was she a honey bee that morning
buzzing between her juniper hive and
daffodils happy to oblige her tongue

be still – don't move around so much
was she a high flying dragon, eager
mistress of all she surveyed as she
built her first castle in the air

see what you did – look at the mess you made
crystal atomizers all askew   was she
a chameleon child with fragranced limbs
airborne on a cloud of cologne

stand in front as long as you like, you'll not be served
no one said   but the silence broke flight
the first ice house formed around her wings
her butterfly heart was eight years old

WHEN I WAS JUST A LITTLE GIRL

Childhood often follows you into adult living rooms
musses your hair and smudges your lipstick
causing you to mistake the salad fork for the soup spoon
and commit other misfortunes at odd hours

So, tell us about yourself, who are you really?
where are you from and where are you going?
all those invitations to unveil, disrobe, unburden
at the hint of a lull or the slip of a masque

I never quite know what to say really,
consider summersaulting along the hallway
or skating across the suddenly icy floor
as quickly as pride and agility allow

Shall I talk about the pristine beauty
of the Great Lakes and skim over
satanic vapors from steel mills and iron foundries?

Wax eloquent about woodframe homes
with wide front porches and skirt
the coldness of hardscrabble rooms?

Trill the names of tall evergreens
gracing the landscape and detour around
grimy backyards infested with snakes?

Chatter about fishing with Dad one summer
and sidestep the cancer deaths in a forlorn town
with two rivers running through it?

© 2014 Jeanne Powell

Confirm the authenticity of nuclear families
where parents excelled in harboring shortages
and rationed hugs as well as words?

Tell us, you say, but you don't really want to know
and I say in oh so many words
once upon a time, long ago and far away…

A GOOD CHILD [1997]

how do you bundle love
in a wicker basket
on such a cold morning

old newsprint discarded
on the back porch
of auntie's house

bluebells dancing
on a blanket grandma gave you
the week she died

torn giftwrap
lying in wait
on a closet floor

a note to Pharaoh
written in the warmth
of mother's blood

> *this is Jacob*
> *he is six days old*
> *I cannot keep him*
> *I am only 12*

jack frost glistens
as the mockingbird trills
forget-me-not lingers

how do you bundle love
in a wicker basket
on such a cold morning

PUPPY LOVE
see Jane
see Spot run
see Jane turn away

she disliked that puppy at first sight
they shared a color, honeysuckle brown
what that puppy didn't know, see,
was trouble for sure
dumb little thing full of needy please
has to be fed, and bathed, and loved
both night and day
before that mutt got too much older
somebody ought to teach it some sense

dumb little thing shook and wiggled
all pink tongue and skinny tail
big eyes trailed her every move
shrugging her braids and creasing her brow
she crossed her arms and turned her back
on this messy boarder's wet oatmeal face

her library books stood sentry between
Wonder Woman comics and school assignments
small brown fingers caressed her new hero
Alexander of Macedonia
teacher said he conquered the world
she read how he was never defeated
when he cried one day it was only because
there were no new worlds for him to conquer

she was sure he had no time for puppies

END OF CEREMONY

a daughter in love with life
a father married to time
they board the daily express
bamboo shadows at their sides

she does not notice him
arranges her stylish gear
sharply edged emphatic grace
breathing fire and ice

he cannot stop gazing
spent a lifetime looking
as she slept in her crib, gurgled milk
took first steps into his heart

her every movement challenges
silver bracelets on golden arms
headphones lock in her allegiance
a western world he cannot fathom

the man sits, still as poured tea
aches inside his careworn clothes
bundled rice bowl by his side
memories brimming in his eyes

JOURNEY

the moment my soles touched the tarmac
I did not think of you at all   the old gang
enveloped me in sweet-tasting tavern songs
and marching chants, evoking times when walls
tumbled and dreams lived hard but high up where
all could see and gain the heart they had to have

in honor of my visit we would mourn Plum Street
conjure Canada outlaws,
celebrate Greektown excursions,
recall car treks to Nine Mile Drive along
rock-salted lanes to view Christmas miracles
in the snow   I did not think of you at all

at times a traffic signal took too long to change
and I would see your face in profile on an iced-over
sign warning of washed-out roads or detours just ahead
then friends would turn our car into an evergreen drive
where warmer faces waited to rekindle select days
as is proper on a journey of the heart

once under the weeping willow in Louise's back yard
I thought I saw a wedge from a croquet mallet, faded
paint blending into winter grass barely exposed
but from the porch came shouts reassuring in their
heartiness that hot mulled wine was waiting and so
there was no time to think of you at all

© 2014 Jeanne Powell

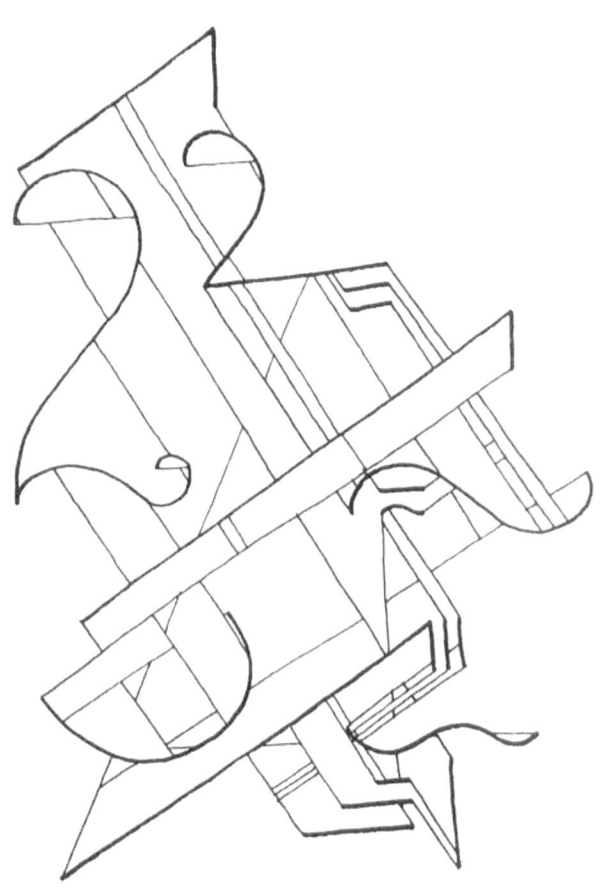

RIBBONS I

what to discard
beach roses
marble lambs
manufactured dreams
hard stone roses
my own silence
blue-daisy dress
sun and shade
music of cicadas
staples of sound
picket fence of pauses
fainting in public
sacred theater
homemade altars
watered dreams
wading to shore
home ground
lacy balconies
freshly squeezed
riverdancing after midnight

RIBBONS II

the unachieved life
prisoner at the bar
mellow asiago
chat the bookie
make a killing
ticket to Mombasa
check the list
lay a false trail
if anyone asks
hosta, phlox & hollyhocks

COFFEE TALK
(reply to an indelicate question about shoes)

scandalous specs fly
among double-espresso and latte-flecked faces
as febrile imaginations turn toward
the closely covered feet
of their merry ringmistress

ever so gently she reminds them
there are moments
when her track and field boots slip off
winsome toes wriggle, wriggle in the warmth
of French syrah and salmon pate'

tawny sundazzle and amazing night glamour
when cranberry satin dominates
the possibilities are infinitely intimate

ever so gently she reminds them…

ON THE WIRE
(utility wires above Market and Church Streets, San Francisco)

It was a party line right from the start
dozens were chirping, heart to heart
the level of glee seemed ecstatic to me
ruffled feathers smoothed without enmity
I was enchanted by the airborne grace
highflying neighbors in energizing song
led me to slow my rushed and hurried pace
and even try to join the singalong

ENTER LAUGHING

A Sunday morning train hurtled across the Bay, while the redhead laughed out loud as she read an article in *Cosmo*. When I sat next to her, we talked about losing weight, and she said she had shed her husband of 22 years. To celebrate, friends had taken her on a tour of sex shops in the City. Retrieving shopping carts at the mall five days a week keeps her tanned and in shape for life's changes. She laughed about painting the ex-husband's name on her favorite vibrator, using nail polish called "kiss my peach." It was a bright beautiful day as I left the train at Pleasant Hill, and the redhead was still laughing.

A WALK IN THE PARK

A clear crisp evening in the park across from a famous cathedral and I admire two burbling fountains attended by miniature bronze nymphs in perpetual play. The attack comes from the rear, a white dog with bushy upturned tail and traveling paws. I squeal, both in fear and from the ignominy of it all. Turning and flailing at manicured paws, I spot the owner nearby, stonefaced in a Navy pea coat. "Would you mind?" I yell, finally finding my voice. The perky white monster trots in the direction of his master's call, then veers off toward one of the fountains. "Blossom!" he calls out again, in a Chinese frame of mind. Blossom scatters in every direction except his. There clearly is no meeting of the minds here, so no malicious intent, I tell myself. Blossom caroms through the park as I contemplate uprooting a cluster of asters and planting them in stoneface's ear.

© 2014 Jeanne Powell

BEANS

leguminous ones
hills and hills
perspicacity
of bushels
filling our lives
with residual
bursts of gratitude
then
a multiplicity of
carbo-oriented
invasions
quinoa
spelt
long-grained wild rice
elbow macaroni
vulgar bulghur
suddenly
our black and brown,
red and green
white and yellow
nurturers are
pushed off
center stage
relegated to
side dishes
and no longer
measure up

WITSTERIA
(to make Angela laugh)

warm windswept rain
wrapped itself wrenchingly
around my withering world

I wailed and walked wearily
through wild wisteria and wet woodchips
in the midst of a Wednesday williwaw

my weeping waned as welcoming friends
wiped my tears and whisked me away
for waffles and wintergreen jam

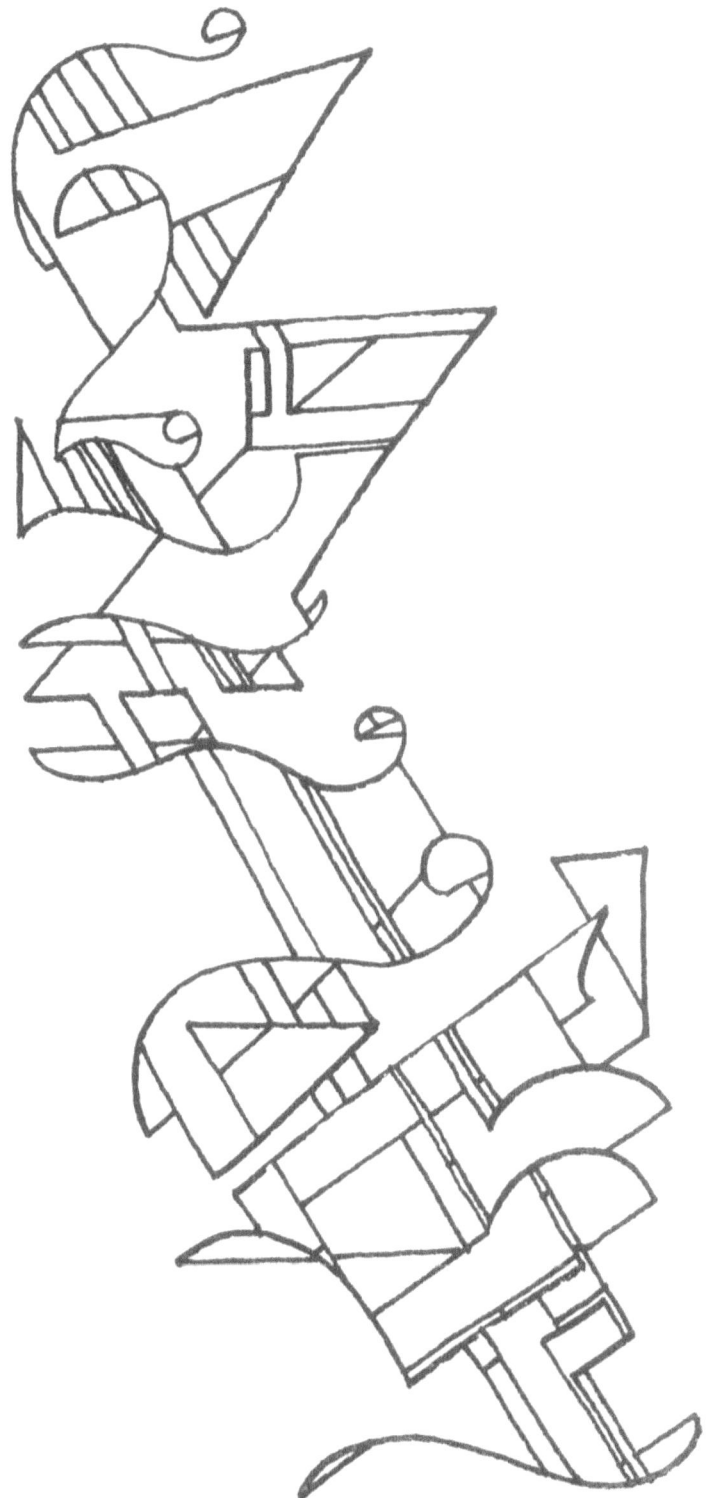

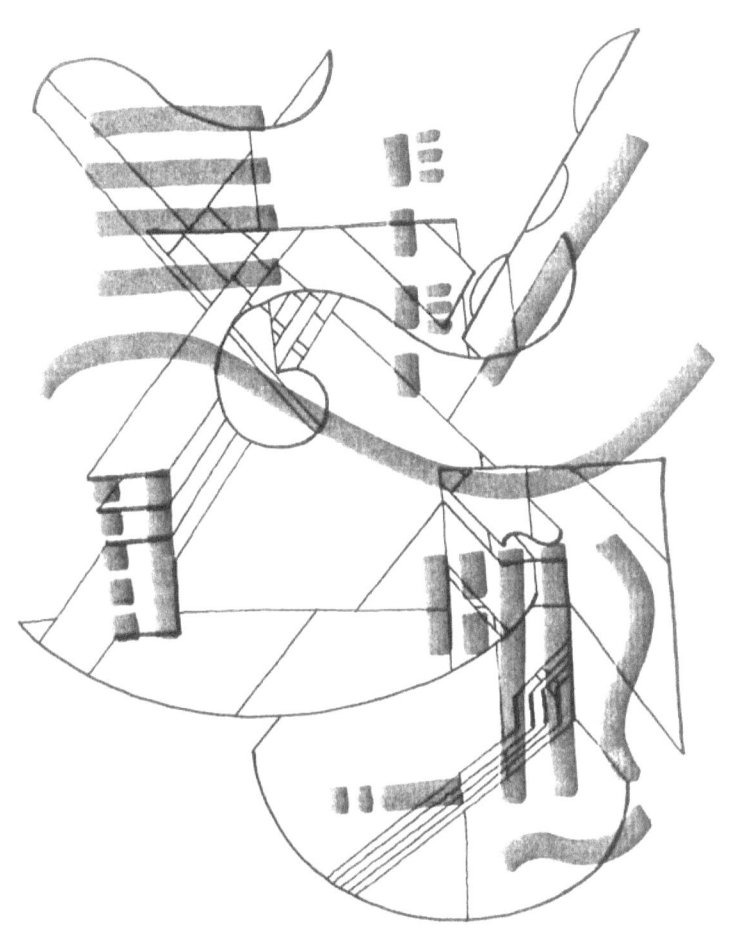

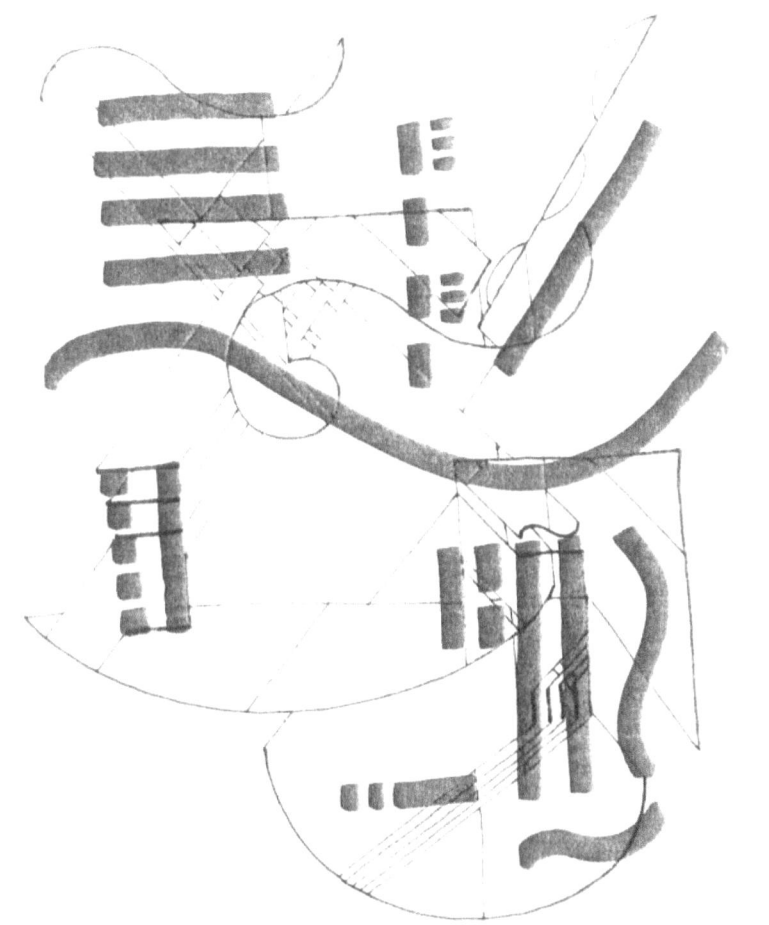

MISLED BY A ROSE

coy as red satin
garnet silhouette
on a silver link fence
she peered through
her own lush foliage
bathed in shimmers of August

who is that flower?
she looks like a vision
we should know and yet…
her petals are single file
did she jettison her petticoats
is she traveling incognita?

no, she's just old fashioned
used to be the one and only
sweet scarlet legend
guile and cunning seduced her
misled her   made her *plush*
it was another century

after all that, she left Verona
the fame and glow of city lights
with steely defiance set up her own
outpost near an underground stream
colors flying single file she was
heard to murmur, *what's in a name*

ROSEMARY

each Tuesday morning, late
on her best blue table
she sets a golden bowl
filled with blood oranges
then flosses her flashing teeth
using mint leaves fresh
from a neighbor's herb garden

promptly at half past two
a gentleman caller arrives
one China rose
cradled in his strong arm
coco plum sweetness
encircling his heart

in her way she is a rosemary
ever green with resurrection
her hopes clustered
as small blue flowers
resolute in the aftermath
of winter

this never-married rose
hedges her bets
all along the coastal byways
sparing neither marsh nor bog
in her eternal quest
for constituent hearts
in a golden bowl

TO STAY THE NIGHT
(in memory of writer Jean Rhys)

tiny fictions
caught in fatal repose
a smile slips
regretful sighs malign
anticipation
polished nails bitten
to the tortured quick
and night has yet to fall

are there midnight options
before the next line
of social embroidery
is sewn to nocturnal hems

a troubled yarn
too often told
such tattered tales!
these threads won't last the night

after leaving Mr. Mackenzie
what is there to do
say good morning to midnight
sleep it off, lady

FIVE O'CLOCK

sunlight in sober retreat,
remorseless, while the woman
lights fires, an unsafe
burning sadly in need
of a chimney sweep's prowl

dust-covered paper set ablaze
frightens ghosts garrulous
before tomorrow's real time
begins another harsh reign
quilted with regrets

petrified flowers fly into
the burning place, lavender love notes
from her choicest blue period,
pieces of heart flash in the flames,
matchbook covers deeply scorched

saffron ribbons tied to summers
past and parched, burn brightly red
tick tock of a wound up clock
five in the morning, five o'clock
long past the grim night of the soul

what, oh what in heaven
is she to do
at five o'clock, tick tock
before morning strikes
what in the world, tick tock
is she to do?

THE LOST PRINCE
(summer 1914)

She dreamed of a brash boy
resolute in a sailor suit
chasing a green parrot, airborne,
along a sunlit hallway
in the summer before the storm,
his leather heels leaving
scuff marks on the polished floor

you'll laugh again, he said
there'll be jolly times
you'll see

DENIAL

too often
a beggar at your door
bare feet
battling
harsh cobblestones
bleeding singsong
hardscrabble dreams
peddler's cart
overturned and bare
a sober offering

I learned
to mince my bites
at your pretty table
not to mar the ambience
with stray tears

after all
frowns from a well-lived
countenance
can devastate
a generation

RED SHOES

enslaved as she is
in past and imperfect time
her origami sensibilities
could go up in flames

persimmons ripen
while this bell-shaped flower
answers the cries of all
who whisper her name

a goddess of mercy
vanishes verily
in swarms of oblong leaves
her red shoes dancing free of blame

CONFESSION

in the summer palace
of the last empress

a thousand dying flowers
a petrified forest

stabs of delight
that fine play of color

small statues of baby Buddha
conceived after death

OLD BELIEVERS

when the edict came
unleashed by heralds
lathered in orthodoxy
Matthew and his brethren
shivered in their new solitude

when the edict came
smothering sweetness in life
widows in name
wept in rude shelters, bracken and
brambles, heather and bilberry

when the edict came
brothers in Christ traveled deep
into forests of aspen and oak,
hawthorne and rowan
to cottages new in their secrecy

when the edict came
Lydia and her sisters
hid in still waters as officials
drew near, hunting monks, hunting
priests, from the old school

*Papal edicts issued in the Middle Ages decreed
that priests and monks must give up marriage*

HISTORY LESSON

unearthed in a Texas museum
two Christian bibles
lovingly bound

in the soft sweet skin
of Comanche mothers
testament to New World blood

the truth will set you free

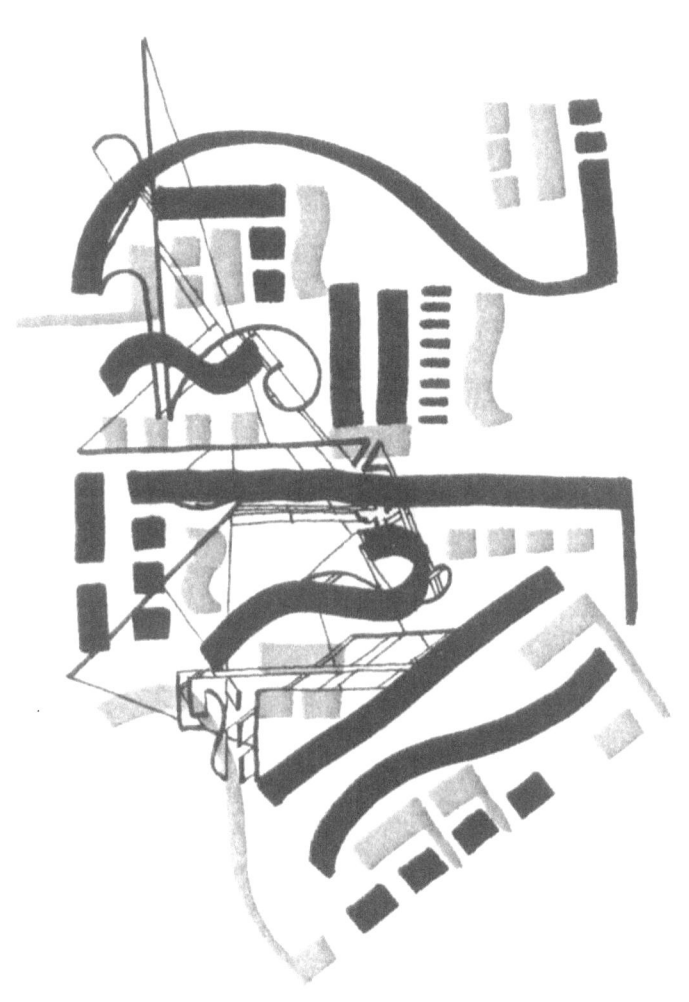

SEPTEMBER 12, 2001
(*a night at the symphony*)

serenade for strings
Opus 48
highlights this evening
anticipation hums from the pit

program in hand
she glides to her tier
long black gown gracing ebony skin
freshwater pearls catch the light

two silver dowagers glance her way
tuck and cover their glittering gems,
then remember where they are
and scrabble for composure

body language smooth as silk,
the newcomer acknowledges
their tarnished smiles,
settles into her seat for the season

silence deepens
lights dim in the gleaming hall
"*same old song,*" she murmurs
as the conductor raises his baton

ORDINARY PEOPLE

That first year in my town's only secondary school, I realized something was different about my family. There was no summer cottage on the lake for us, no graceful sailboat at the end of the pier. We did not winter anywhere except the same clapboard house where I was born and raised. Dandelions brightened our crabgrass parcel in the spring, fireflies lit three-leafed clovers every summer, falling leaves decorated our weathered porch late in autumn, a full panoply of snowflakes danced on the ramshackle roof when winter came. There was nothing gourmet about Dicers Market where my mother shopped, nothing grand about fresh goat roasting on a spit near my father's union hall every Fourth of July.

Years passed and from the four corners of the earth we returned to our town with two separate bridges to a foreign country. Class reunion. Over aperitifs and hors d'oeuvres I watched and listened, my yearbook memories forever colored by this new education. There are worse things than threadbare carpets and empty cupboards, worse things than powdered eggs reconstituted on Easter morning, worse things than Salvation Army baskets on porches Christmas Eve.

You know those glass-paneled homes on Amber Lane and Azure Cove? My glittering classmates spoke of fathers in the wrong bedroom after dark. They spoke of expensive whiskey bottles empty too often, suicide dreams from which no one woke, and scarlet letters in the afterglow.

I won't throw stones, but I wish someone had
for the people I used to know.

SUNSET BAR

Late one autumn Saturday we were sitting on a plump sofa in a Sunset bar David had chosen, positioned nicely in front of the woodburning fireplace, about to snuggle, when a man and woman walked through the double doors. At first I barely noticed but they paused, longer than necessary, to survey the candlelit room and choose where they would sit. Eventually I turned my attention from the always mysterious David, and gazed at them.

You could say she was the color of chestnuts roasting on an open fire, as David once described me, but there the similarity ended. Her makeup was noticeable, as were the years she tried to hide, not so much the years, but their impact on her. The man was a bit unsteady on his feet at this hour, but amiable and familiar in his attentiveness. What drew my attention was the way she seemed to freeze when she caught sight of me.

David made a rare comment not in response to anything I had said, and I encouraged him with a dazzling smile, my dark curly hair tumbling around my bare shoulders. The couple still stood just inside the swinging doors, while the woman looked at me, stared as though she had no other choice. I checked to see if I knew her, but realized I did not.

A crackling log flared in the fireplace; I saw her clearly then and she observed me. The woman's jaw seemed to sag and slow tears glistened in bloodshot eyes. David was telling me how he discovered this pub right after returning from Ireland, while his eyes narrowed and flicked over the woman in turmoil and the ruddy drunk whose arm was comfortably around her shoulder. "Wassa matter, babe? Don't you like this place anymore? Where you wanna sit?"

The man chose a table nearby and with elaborate gestures held a chair for his companion. He lit a Marlboro for her. A barmaid approached and took their order. The woman's eyes never left me. Full in the moment of my joyous youth and David's sober courtship, I shrugged away her February face. Part of me knew this was not about me or the Sunset bar. Part of me stood away, near the fireplace mantle and observed a phenomenon, that of time, which takes on everyone, like James Brown said in a song lyric. I was young and strong, and no Sampson had cut my long hair. So there was time still, you see.

IF THE SHOE FITS

buying a new pair of shoes
second nature
nothing to fear
get on the bus
sit next to the driver
walk into the mall
find a comfortable chair
signal a clerk
wait for the right fit
piece of cake, easy as pie

my father he bought shoes
through mail order
Sears Roebuck's Wish Book
'cause you couldn't try them on
in any store he knew
guess somebody heard about it
finally did something
Capitol Hill
the White House
maybe the Supreme Court

suddenly
you could go downtown
walk into retail
sit on a naugahyde chair
and try some on for size
one thing, though
nobody told the tightlipped clerk
about service with a smile

imagine, if you will
dressed in your best brown skin
and shiniest braids
trying on patent leather and maryjanes
under the flinty gaze
of one who last visited
your neighborhood in the moonlight
dressed all in white
America, where all things are possible…

NEXT TIME
(*a meditation on ancestral memories*)

wading into reflections
immersed in the roar of the crowd
free Cathy walked toward the center of the earth
lowered her torch to the still waters
ignited a running ring
the firedance surrounded her
please do not let them burn her

logic said they left her a way to escape
they won't burn her she's their only
Aboriginal symbol
pioneer and champion
reason replied they burn symbols have
incinerated pioneers may sacrifice champions
do not let them burn her

she would make such a glowing sacrifice
consecrate the games fire their spirits
purify the hemorraging history of
Down Under's new world order
so brave   her grace in silent
running waves all around her
do not let them burn her

a sly miracle woman
she escaped the burning
stepped clear of the ring
leaving the fire this time
and faced the arena
where the crowd waited
for the games to begin

© 2014 Jeanne Powell

EAST BAY MIRACLE
(Oakland CA 1993)

Televersion burbles
fact-based images
penetrating mind wombs
with shotgun precision
until an implant
mushrooms into a life term

shot while thieving
sad-eyed woman
pregnant with failure
lingers in dead zone limbo
pinned by surprise
three times running—
semen, bullets, medical circus

newspeak trumpets
mother-to-be
dead to the world
barren of power
strapped in twilight
let go a living child
while men in white
immerse themselves
in the afterbirth of glory

the Lazarus experts
bundle their orphan
their Caesarian find
to the welfare network
on primetime schedule

from grave to cradle
better living
through competition
for the best experiments
in Black

A TRUE STORY

young and black he was in search of trouble
old and rich she seemed a likely victim
disgorged by the subway train
into her flowerbox neighborhood
trimmed with sweet pea and Italian crocus.
he followed in alien terrain, risking more than he knew
for a dead alligator with gold handles.
grabbing and running, holding the bag, he did not get far.
cognoscenti flew out of flowerboxes
exploded from chairs in corner cafes
took the guilty youth to the highest rooftop
tipped him expertly over the gargoyle edge
for the short flight to oblivion
and returned the purse to her with apologies.
local constabulary agreed the punishment fit the crime
low volume news coverage here   it was understood
this East Coast neighborhood policed itself.
just suppose—
for a moment—
this avenue was in the middle of Oakland,
a bakery on the corner sold sweet potato pies,
and a mosque nestled among single-family homes.
if some towheaded teen ripped off a woman's purse
and the brothers flew *him* off the nearest tall building
can you picture CBS news dropping this story
on the cutting room floor
or the local police filing this felony with unsolved crimes?
me neither…*this*
is a true story

LAST CALL

Sunday in the park near St. Peter and St. Paul
I read a syndicated column in the Chronicle.
Pete Hamill wrote about the amnesty–
American stowaway jumped ship in India,
wed an older woman and fathered five kids
as he waited for the chance to come home.

Your Gioconda smile, those raw sienna eyes
fired by dreams of Che and Fidel, the poetry of
Ho Chi Minh in a French prison–was it
Hong Kong or Stockholm shielding you
from the long reach of our red squads
while you waited for the chance to come home?

As we raised money for the Cause and spread the word,
you appeared 'round midnight after the dilettantes had gone.
devouring spaghetti and red wine, you revived our spirits
when all seemed futile, a gentle masculine version of
La Pasionaria in Madrid–"*No pasaran, no pasaran!*"
the enemy is coming. we shall NOT be moved.

That curly black beard, you looked like Jesus, did I ever tell you?
when you disappeared we did not know right away
it was normal for you to be underground;
the Railroad had been revived.
a very long cold winter, then handmade markers
glistened under slippery ice. a body count
revealed many missing in action that year.

© 2014 Jeanne Powell

Dispatches from the other side hinted amnesty was in the air.
we looked for you, knowing you might come in disguise
to examine the terrain. assassins were everywhere–
agents provocateur, red squads, needles filled with white death,
birds on the wire. was that your coat blowing in the wind,
your car running on empty, your Gioconda smile in the poison
rain?

ON SARAJEVO TIME
1992-1995

slowing my steps
I looked softly
at roses, tulips, lilies
brightening the kiosk.
dressed in ashes of twilight,
a ghost of a man emerged.
blood fragments clung to his irises
snapdragons drove away the sun
but he still lived.
together we leaned toward explosions of color,
selected a single, solitary stem.
he dressed it lovingly in shrouds of fern,
presented the flower with a formal bow.
so it began, this morning ritual
against a backdrop of concrete and steel
wondrously intact,
and citizens who walked upright.
each morning I read the screaming headlines
before approaching the kiosk,
that summer of neighbor killing neighbor,
of Christians slaughtering Muslims.
then one day he said,
I am going home
my city is alive again.
he hoped to see rosemary, juniper and laurel
near the many new graveyards
he would look for the oak near the mosque
and the café in the square
a flower in the rubble
and hope in his prayers.

© 2014 Jeanne Powell

TROUBLE IN MIND

wasabi darkness
family of tornadoes
war bedevilled citizens
what is there to celebrate?
once we dreamed of reconciliation
now we cannot fathom
your sense of loss
you cannot penetrate our blindness.
armies are massing.
somebody gestures from a distance
any threat is an affirmation
our budget is ripe and bursting.
the British greased bullets with tallow
and Hindus mutinied at Sepoy.
we slime the rockets with bacon
the better to anger Allah.
nothing personal, this wholesale destruction.
it grows normal to bathe
in the blood of our prime-time enemies.

POSTMORTEM 2000

November was in an ugly state that year.
A Florida brunette stripteased and rode the airwaves
for days on end, petulant and pouting. Her chads
undulated with a fierce promiscuity until
national eardrums burst from funereal sobs of longing.
Our constitutional façade collapsed in tainted shreds,
creating abominal snow on America's television
screens. Grand Old Party celebrants circledanced
in patriotic Gore, leaving indelible footprints.
Swamplands dried up from heated flag waving,
revealing the corpses of would-be voters buried in
white lies, red tape and wintry blues.
I promised you law, not justice,
intoned an adjudicating giant from a distant past.
Is the old jurist turning in his courtly grave,
now that we have neither?

© 2014 Jeanne Powell

NOVEMBER 3, 2004
(around 12:00 noon)

what you see is me crouching
I need to examine the terrain
assess the strength of my enemy
I may roll over and play dead
hug a low-slung tree limb for hours
crawl through the debris
of your preoccupation with self
without leave or portfolio
my agenda is anything but simple.
somebody, help me!

MAKING AMENDS

1
arms
you
are you experienced?
men at arms
women in arms
have you the right?
arm youself
you had rights once
forearmed
is forewarned

2
you have
the right
to bare all
heart, soul, spleen
you have
the right
to bare
bloodstained teeth
in silent witness
as the horror unfolds

3
you have
the right
to bear up
under heavy water
as patriotic armadillos
rain down
weapons of mass destruction

4
you have
the right
to hunt bear
in season
polar and Kodiak and Wall Street
using your own pearl-handled
grenade launcher

5
you have
the right
to call to arms and legs
breasts and hips
thighs and lips
for comfort
during unfriendly fire

6
you have
the right
to bear
any burden
pay any price
for a Remington or
Winchester experience

7
you have
the right
to bare arms, naked
upper extremities
waxed free
of offending hair follicles

8
you have
the right
to bear arms
in the household of another
to punish
ungrateful colonists
who commit treason
against the Crown
against the New World Order

9
you
have rights
still
you think?
barely visible
mostly
in your dreams

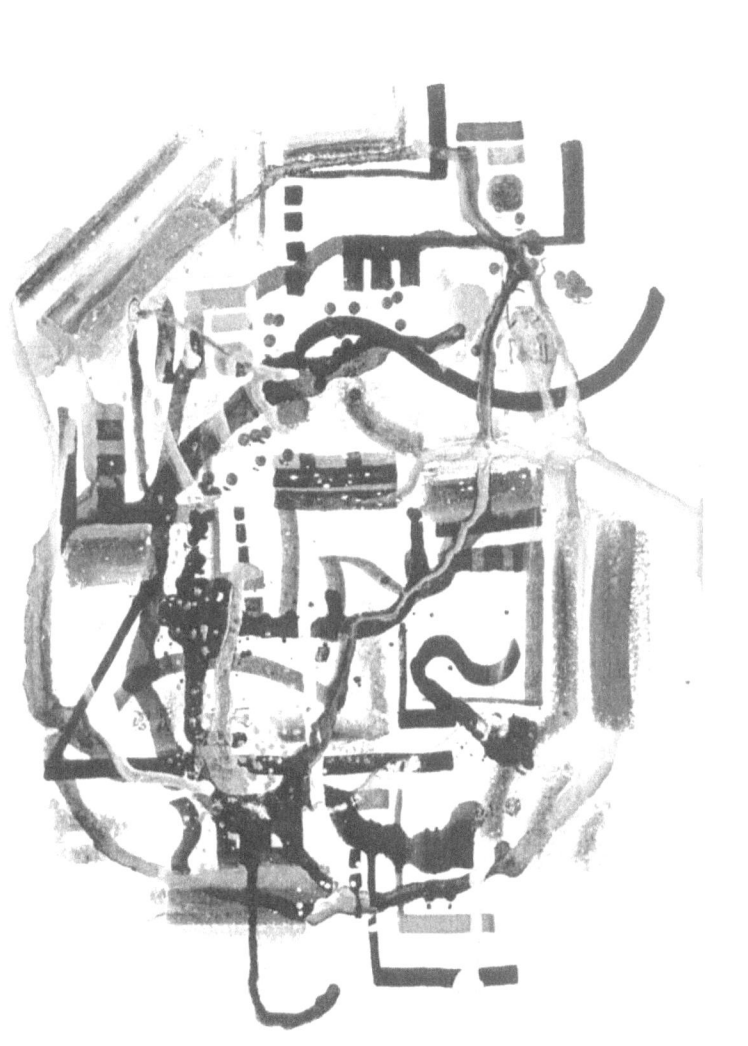

THIS IS A LOVE POEM

in my hand a crumpled page
sprung from stillness
no story, this
listen for the song inside

a love poem unwritten till now
there was no time, you see, and no reason
after all, you died before I was born
in my story
and I fell in love at your grave

a love poem
the one you wrote before I could read
the one I spoke before you could hear
so the story goes

this poem was whispered
as midnight tolled
in a guarded fortress
one candle illuminating
walls of armor

one afternoon a friend called
come to Hollywood, he said,
write your own script
the weather will be sizzling
leave your armor at the bus stop

a poem from one warrior
to another, in loving spirit
good game, high stakes
I've got the right stuff
and a new contract

now I know I can sing and dance
any time, every day
this crumpled page?
Oh—this is a love poem

A GRATITUDE POEM
(*July 2004*)

I embody divine expression
coming as I do from a far country
where people dream in cypress groves
and compose cinnamon poems
waist high in the blazing sun

Teacher took us through
strange unsanitary landscapes
rough with memory and emotion
in good and imperfect time

There was a chance we would die dancing
or go up in flames
instead we unearthed courage
to listen for the song inside

Now we grow lush and green
spruce and tamarack and poplar
recreating every day
and our hair fills up with butterflies

© 2014 Jeanne Powell

WAR *HAIKU*

1

twin towers blasted
from that Big Apple skyline
innocence has fled

2

Afghani winters
for invaders seeking spoils
centuries of defeat

3

a crimson sunset
night fires burning till dawn
Afghanistan bleeds

4

brilliant red poppies
adorn the freshly turned earth
home is the warrior

5

wide young eyes harvest
grief etched in a widow's gaze
the last full measure

© 2014 Jeanne Powell

1
henna markings sweet,
red, wild, my name in your hands
your name in my heart

2
untamed lavender
deep in the Persian mountains
tempting you to pray

3
homemade altars
watered dreams
sacred theater

1
raindrops caress red
blooms on winter windowsills
all seasons court love

2
Mikimoto pearls
encircling breakfast croissants
early signs of love

1
this is who I am
fully alive and vibrant
be it ever so

2
there are no roads here
you make your path as you go
hardy voyager

3
high atop green hills
we shall toast life's sweet rewards
with cups of wry tears

1
tangerine season
when all the tart slices lay
seige to your taste buds

2
blue daisy dress
riverdancing after midnight
music of cicadas

3
fat mourning doves
cuddle in a walnut tree
squirrels scamper below

1
she has the courage
to show you things you don't know
imagination

2
mother finds child
daydreaming on kitchen floor
and mops around her

1
so much pain inside
why struggle to keep it close
because it is mine

2
what you harbor now
did not transpire at all
but then, you know that

1
camellia branches
lament these sun-raptured days
brittle buds cry, "rain!"

2
rain-splattered crystal
prisms scatdance with treetops
hailstorm at midnight

1
flutes dance with Taiko
rhythmic pounding of rice cakes
Japanese *mochi*

2
bonfire flaring
bare feet dancing on the sand
celebrate autumn

1
sweet apricot dawn
such possibilities die
with a blood orange moon

2
on the frozen grave
we prayed to anything
that might exist

3
too cautious to shine
the sun still has not risen
bleak faith lies frozen

1
solemn harvest moon
illuminates our grief
this frosty autumn

2
oak trees shiver now
that autumn rattles boldly
through their sturdy limbs

1
marigolds and onions
keep your garden safe from pests
when will you plant them

2
friends of green and black
shower me with wet tea leaves
a new way to drink

3
colorful displays
cornucopia of bargains
the joy of Trader Joe's

4
life in Port Huron
roller skates and penny sweets
memories stream by

1
guardians in her
tiara balance the queen
majestic strolling

2
store in a cold place
slowcook without defrosting
would Martha approve?

3
Martha firmly folds
fitted sheets so they lie flat
tyranny at home

4
eggs broken, toast burned
peaches bruised and abandoned
family reunion

1
scraps of white lace duel
with random hopes of color
her fear of winter

2
incivility
hidden in a lotus marsh
pretty blooms conceal

3
hooded white falcon
jessied in scarlet, tightens
his grip on her wrist

1
neither mushrooms nor moss
obscure Nature's true beauty
tears gilding moonlight

2
pungent wild fennel
parsley sage rosemary thyme
seasoned favorites

3
foam-capped ocean waves
snowladen mountain valleys
Nature's formal wear

1
newsprint carnivores
truth censored for the right price
Fourth Estate in decay

2
I've watched presidents
die and that is why your lies
will not defeat me

BIRDS

1
tradewind travelers
form ribbons on air currents
heroic journey

2
sparrows, blackbirds, hawks
maneuver as seasons change
airborne pilgrimage

3
cooper's hawk, laughing
gull, cormorant, naked man
summer birdwatching

4
razorbills resting
on our pond, no need to freeze
birding in winter

5
predatory gulls
kill migratory songbirds
oh, murder most foul!

1
blue haiku ribbons
dance across a kiwi sky
live animation

2
rainbow kimonos
flash in flurries of movement
the clamor of spring

3
capricious breezes
fuzzy dandelion seeds
delicious movement

A MEDITATION WITH DOROTHY AND HER FRIENDS

1

polished stone vibrates
I sit in a wicker chair
hearing its music

2

berry-red petals
cluster on devoted stems
peony beauty

3

lilies pale long-stemmed
adorn an earthenware bowl
a gift to Spirit

4

walking in wet sand
offering copper pennies
the ocean accepts

5

rose quartz blushes
emerging from centuries
of hibernation

© 2014 Jeanne Powell

1
voyager raindrops
playfully birdtracking each
well-traveled window

2
organic love, free
of all known toxicity
except the wanting

ABOUT THE AUTHOR

Jeanne Powell has earned degrees from WSU in Detroit and USF in San Francisco. She writes prose poems, flash fiction and short stage plays. Her books include MY OWN SILENCE and WORD DANCING, both published in second editions by Taurean Horn Press in 2013/2014. For ten years Jeanne hosted an acclaimed spoken word series, "Celebration of the Word." She is the inspiration behind Meridien PressWorks™ which has published 20 authors since 1996. She has been an instructor in the CS, OLLI and UB programs in California.

FEBRUARY VOICES
"She writes…with the honesty of a survivor and the elegance of a stylist. Whether satirizing…or keening…or offering her own story with irony and gracefulness, her *Voices* are promising poems. I recommend that readers read them, and recommend that she write more."
                            Christopher Bernard
                            Editor, *Caveat Lector*

CADENCES
"*Cadences* is an impressive collection that fulfills the promise of *February Voices,* drawing us into its rhythms and meanings on many levels. These poems…sing and rage in ways that are compelling, enchanting and unforgettable."
                            Dr. Louise M. Jefferson
                            Wayne State University

MY OWN SILENCE

"*My Own Silence* is a testament against the worst type of silence—that of indifference. These are poems of conscience in which the poet ends her silence by transforming her outrage into unforgettable images… Yet, despite the world's cruelty and sorrows, the poet finds much in which she can rejoice…This is a book that looks hard at life…and embraces it in all its complexity."

> Lucille Lang Day, Ph.D.
> Author of *Wild One* and *Infinities*

"*My Own Silence* is a vibrant, cohesive collection of story poems, with bold beginnings and endings neatly tucked. The writer spins dramatic filaments into poetic gold with a rhythmic ear and a robust voice. Cousin to Whitman, Jordan, Collins—Jeanne Powell's literary threads are expertly woven into America's tapestry of struggle and redemption."

> Stephen Kopel
> Author of *Spritz*

At a time when the confessional mode has banished American poetry to one vast self-mirroring island, the work of Jeanne Powell nudges us again and again to break out of our little selves. Whether celebrating the triumphs of Australia's champion Aboriginal athlete Cathy Freeman, berating a hellish vacation in the Sierra Foothills, disclosing the subtle and not so subtle pain of social injustice, or commemorating a powerful, dancing mother reared in the big band swing era, Powell rocks. Unfailingly, the open-hearted spirit of her prose and poetry allows us to re-experience our membership in one another.

— **AL YOUNG,** *California Poet Laureate Emeritus*

www.ingramcontent.com/pod-product-compliance
Lightning Source LLC
Chambersburg PA
CBHW030447300426
44112CB00009B/1199